In the Garden of our Minds

and
other Buddhist stories

Blue Moon Aurora, LLC
Silver Spring, MD
www.bluemoonaurora.com
For ordering and additional book information, visit http://50percentdakini.com

First edition
Printed in the United States of America

Publisher's Cataloging-in-Publication data
Johnson-Weider, Michelle Lynn.
    In the garden of our minds and other Buddhist stories / written by Michelle L. Johnson-Weider ; illustrated and graphic design by Brian Chen.
    p. cm.
    ISBN 978-0-9837984-6-0
    Summary : A modern Western family with two rambunctious young children uses traditional Buddhist stories and simple mindfulness practices to help cope with everyday problems and fears.

[1. Buddhism --Fiction. 2. Religious life --Buddhism --Fiction. 3. Short stories, American.] I. Chen, Brian S. II. Title.

PZ7.J63415 In 2013
[Fic] --dc23

2013902707

Dedication

To my one and only and always love, Kirk, for supporting all of my endeavors; to my parents, Gene and Terry Johnson, for taking me to Nepal where I first encountered Tibetan Buddhism; to my children, Anton Alexander and Alina Bryseis, who inspired me to write this book; and above all to Bardor Tulku Rinpoche, who performed my refuge ceremony on March 20, 1996, and Garchen Rinpoche, who performed Alina's on January 17, 2010.

May I be free from suffering.

May my family be free from suffering.

May all sentient beings be free from suffering.

Buddhist books are most beneficial and precious to educate children. The Buddha himself said, 'in the degenerate age in the future I will appear in the form of scriptures.' Without books to learn we could not develop our understanding and wisdom. There are many virtuous activities and some of the most beneficial are to write texts, to translate texts, to recite texts, to give texts, etc. To offer learning to a child is much more beneficial than material things. If you give them some money, they will be happy temporarily, but then again the money will be used up and may even cause harm. Through books we do not only learn for this life but we also cultivate wisdom for future lives. When children read a book, it leaves an imprint in their mind, thus to teach them the dharma through books plants a seed of liberation in their minds.

It is extremely important and beneficial to teach children when they are young; in this way they will form good habits for their entire life. For this reason I am very grateful to you for producing such a book.

March 23, 2012

His Eminence Garchen Rinpoche

is a Drikung Kagyu lama who was reconized
and enthroned in eastern Tibet by the former
Drikung Kyabgon Zhiwe Lodro.
Garchen Rinpoche is the founder and spiritual director of
the Garchen Buddhist Institute in
Chino Valley, Arizona (www.garchen.net).

As the Western sangha grows, we must look at how to support families in their practice and study of the Buddhist path. This is especially important for families with young children. In today's world, we need loving and compassionate families who can help their children lead a life of kindness. The teachings of the Buddha are especially relevant in this context. Western society may not always offer a strong level of support for Buddhist practice and so we must work together to strengthen the sangha. That process begins with how we help our children assimilate Buddhist values into their worldview.

Michelle L. Johnson-Weider's book, In the Garden of our Minds and other Buddhist stories, provides a wonderful way to introduce Buddhist ideals to young children. Her stories, told with love and humor, introduce us to the family of Alex and Briana. Through the many dilemmas they face, we can see how the teachings of the Buddha can help us in everyday life. In addition to the stories, Michelle has included discussion questions, "Conversations with Children," so families can further explore the lessons offered in the stories. My hope is that with stories like these we can help families, especially those with young children, live with compassion and, in that way, build a strong Western sangha.

March 1, 2012   Bardor Tulku

Bardor Tulku Rinpoche

was recognized by the 16th Karmapa, Rangjung Rigpe
Dorje, as the 3rd incarnation of Terchen Barway Dorje.
Rinpoche has lived and taught in the United States for over
thirty years. He is the founder and spiritual director of
Kunzang Palchen Ling, a Tibetan Buddhist center in Red
Hook, NY (www.kunzang.org).

Acknowledgements

The author would like to thank Ina Bieler and Basia Coulter for their invaluable assistance. Thank you to Mary Ruth Blackwell Coleman, Lisa Lewis, and Anne C. Lewis for graciously reviewing the manuscript and providing valuable feedback. Darcie Chan reviewed an early draft and was supportive throughout. Terry Johnson's enthusiastic proof-reading and Kirk Johnson-Weider's assistance at every step of the way have made the publication of this book a reality. Finally, I extend my heartfelt thanks to Brian Chen, whose gorgeous illustrations brought my words to life.

Table of Contents

Prince Siddhartha
Renounces The Throne

The golden sun of late afternoon shone down warmly on the two children running across the yard. "You can't catch me!" yelled the little girl as she fled merrily from her older brother, who had a handful of red and brown leaves ready to throw if he could just get close enough. Their smiles faded as they heard their mother call from the front door. "Alex, Briana, time to come in and do your homework!"

"Oh please, Mama," pleaded Briana. "Just five more minutes?"

"This is the second 'just five more minutes' you've had today," Mama said. "It's getting late and you've got to get your work done before dinner. Come on in."

Alex threw down the leaves and stomped toward the house. "I hate homework," he grumbled. "I wish it was still summer and we could play all the time."

"If you get your homework done quickly, you might have some more time to play," suggested Mama.

"Not likely," Alex complained. "After homework, I'll have to set the table and then it'll be dinner and then shower and then bed! There's never enough time."

"I wish we could play all day long and all night too!" cried Briana as she twirled in a pile of fallen leaves.

"Me too," said Alex. "But parents don't let their kids just play. It's always work, work, work."

Mama laughed. "Come on, you two. I'll tell you what. If you hurry up inside and get your homework done, I'll tell you a story before dinner, a story about a father who forced his son to play all the time."

"No way," said Alex. "I'll bet he was the happiest kid on earth!"

"Not exactly," said Mama. "In fact, he was quite miserable."

She held the door open and the children entered. "I doubt he was miserable," said Alex.

"Finish your homework and you can find out," Mama told him.

"Okay, okay - I'll get my homework done quickly today!"

"That would be a nice change," Mama said with a smile.

An hour later, both children were curled up on the couch next to their mother, who began her story. "A long time ago, there was a prince born in what is now Nepal."

Briana frowned. "Stories are supposed to begin with 'once upon a time', Mama."

"Fairy stories, yes," agreed Mama. "But this isn't a fairy story. This is a true story."

"Really?" asked Alex, sitting up and looking more interested. "How long ago did it happen?"

"About two thousand five hundred years ago," Mama continued. "Now, when this prince was born, a wise man came to see the child.

'What can you tell me about my son?' the king demanded. 'Will he be a great king like me?'

'Perhaps,' said the wise man as he peered at the beautiful baby boy. 'Perhaps he will be an even greater king than you or any other king who has ever lived. Or perhaps he will renounce the throne and pursue the holy life in order to free all living beings from

suffering. In that case, he will be one of the greatest spiritual leaders that the world has ever known.'"

"What does 'renounce' mean?" asked Briana.

"It means to give something up," Mama explained. "So if you renounce the throne, you give it up - you say that you don't want to be king anymore."

"Wait a minute," said Alex. "What was the prince's name?"

"He was named Siddhartha, which means 'one who achieves his goal'."

"I knew it!" exclaimed Alex. "This is the story of the Buddha, isn't it?"

"That's right," Mama said. "But before Siddhartha became Gautama Buddha, he was a prince who lived a life of perfect luxury."

"That must have been nice," said Briana enviously.

"I'm sure it was. The king was so worried that Siddhartha would see the suffering in the world and renounce the throne that he gave his son everything he could wish for: the best food to eat, the most beautiful dancers to entertain him, never-ending music and games, even entire pleasure palaces to live in - one for each season. And the king gave strict orders that no one who was sick or old or suffering in any way was allowed to come near the prince."

"Did he have to do homework?" asked Alex.

"And chores?" asked Briana.

Mama laughed. "The king ordered everything arranged so that the prince would always be happy and would never think of renouncing worldly life. His teachers made his schoolwork like a

game and there were always people ready to divert him if he started to get bored. Yet despite all of this, the prince was not content."

"Why not?" demanded Alex. "He had everything he could ever wish for!"

"True, but having lots of things and lots of diversions doesn't bring lasting happiness. Maybe it was fun while he was a boy, but eventually Prince Siddhartha began to feel that there must be more to life than just playing all the time. His father tried all sorts of things to divert Siddhartha, even arranging his marriage to a beautiful young woman. However, Prince Siddhartha still was not content and begged his father to let him go out into the city so that he could see how other people lived."

"Did his papa agree?" asked Briana.

"Well, the king wasn't happy about the idea," said Mama, "but he didn't want to refuse his son. He arranged for a great festival so that when Siddhartha left the palace all he would see were beautiful things - happy people, clean streets, and endless celebration. But of course it's a lot more difficult to control a whole city than it is to control a pleasure palace."

"I know this part of the story," said Alex. "When the prince left the palace he saw four different people: one sick person, one old person, one dead person, and one monk."

"That's right," said Mama. "Siddhartha had never seen anything like the four sights before and they bothered him deeply. For the first time, he learned that it is in the nature of all beings to sicken, grow old, and eventually die. For the first time, he knew that all of these things would happen to him too, no matter how much his father tried to protect him. But when Siddhartha saw the holy man, he also realized that some people were trying to find release from suffering. So he decided to renounce his royal birth forever and find a way to help all people be free from suffering."

"Just like the wise man had said!" exclaimed Briana. "So did he do it? Did he leave the palace?"

"Yes, he did," said Mama. "He left in the middle of the night with only his faithful servant Channa. When they had traveled a distance from the palace, Siddhartha cut his long hair and took off all of his expensive jewels. He told Channa to take everything back to the palace and tell the king that he had gone to find the way to end all suffering."

"The king must have been really sad," said Briana.

"He definitely was. So were Siddhartha's wife and everyone else in the palace! They couldn't understand how someone who had every possible pleasure could give it all up to take on the very difficult job of ending suffering."

"I don't get it either," said Alex. "I would've stayed and just played all day long."

Mama smiled and gave him a hug. "Well, I'm glad that you're not ready to leave home quite yet, though you're quite a bit younger than Siddhartha was when he decided that he was tired of being confined in the pleasure palaces all the time. He was almost 30 years old and his father still wasn't letting him make decisions about his life! Siddhartha had realized that even if he spent his whole life

in the palaces, he couldn't escape sickness, old age, and death. Not only that, but he couldn't protect his father, his wife, his child, or any of his other loved ones from suffering the same fate. Life in the palaces might be a lot of fun for a while, but eventually everyone would face these three inevitable problems and Siddhartha wasn't about to just sit back and let that go on happening."

"So did it work?" asked Briana. "Did he find a way to end suffering?"

"Of course he did!" said Alex. "That's how he became the Buddha, remember? If he hadn't become enlightened, he wouldn't have been able to teach Buddhism and then we wouldn't be Buddhist!"

Mama laughed. "That's one way of looking at it."

"Can you tell us the rest of what happened after Siddhartha left the palace?" Briana pleaded.

"Another time. Right now, I have to help Papa with dinner and Alex needs to set the table."

"I wish I was a prince in a pleasure palace," groaned Alex.

"Maybe you were in a previous life," Mama said. "But right now you're a boy with chores to do."

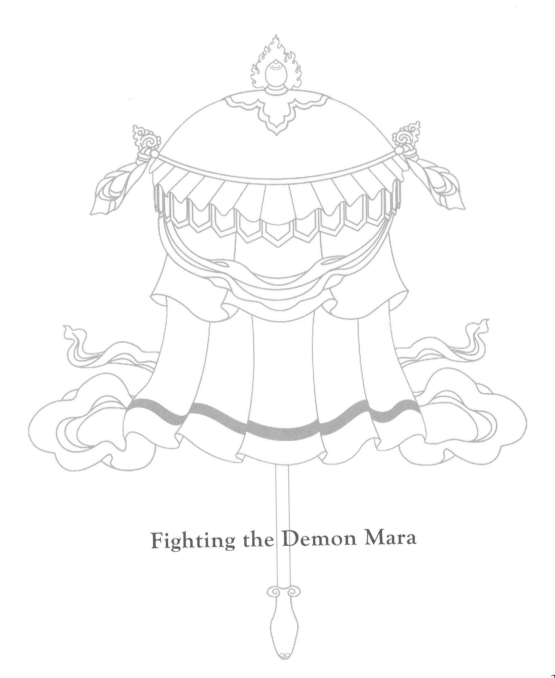

Fighting the Demon Mara

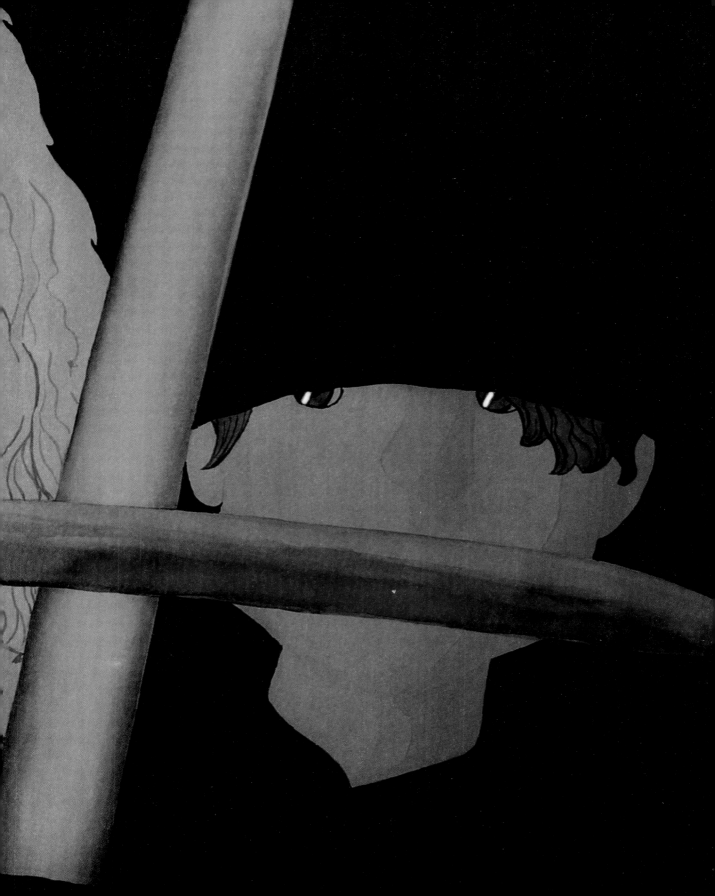

Mama and Papa were curled up on the couch with their favorite books and a cat each, when Alex and Briana burst into the room. Briana brandished a sword while twirling her flowered cape. Alex flourished a lightsaber from beneath a hooded robe.

"Yes?" said Papa, looking up from his book.

"We are Capewoman and the Black Ranger!" cried Briana.

"We are brave warriors who have fought many demons," said Alex. "Now we are hunting the greatest of all evildoers - the demon Mara. Have you seen him?"

"Actually, yes," said Mama. "I saw him this morning."

"You did?" yelled Briana. "Where? Capewoman and the Black Ranger will destroy him!"

"He was at breakfast," said Mama.

"What?" asked Alex. "I didn't see him."

"It was when Papa told Briana to set the table and she started to get the silverware out. You went to get napkins and Briana shouted that it was her job and she hit you. I saw Mara then."

The children were quiet for a moment.

"And I saw Mara last night," Papa said.

"Really?" Alex's eyes opened wide.

"Yep, at dinner. It was when there was only one piece of lasagna left and Alex started eating really quickly so he could get it before Briana. Then, once he got it, he was too full to finish."

"You're right," agreed Mama. "I saw Mara then too."

Alex lowered his lightsaber and put his arm around Mama. "So we are Mara?" he asked.

Mama smiled. "There's some of Mara in each of us," she said.

"Even you?" asked Briana, coming closer and petting the cats.

"Even me," said Mama. "Remember the other night when I came home from work and you wanted to show me the picture you'd drawn and Alex wanted me to read his new library book, and I shouted at everyone to be quiet and leave me alone? I definitely saw Mara then."

"So what is Mara?" asked Alex. "Is he really a demon?"

"Mara is a name we give to the emotions that make it hard for us to do the right thing," said Mama. "Emotions like anger, pride, selfishness, jealousy, greed, and doubt. Sometimes they are called poisons or the afflictive emotions. We make Mara real when we act on those emotions."

"But didn't Mara fight the Buddha?" asked Briana.

"Well, he tried to," smiled Mama. "Do you remember the story? It was many years after Prince Siddhartha had left his palace home. He'd been practicing long and hard to find a way to end all suffering. He had studied with many different teachers and tried many difficult ascetic practices, and finally realized that he needed to seek a middle way, some technique in between the indulgences of the pleasure palaces and the strict asceticism of the many wandering holy men. Finally, Siddhartha arranged a cushion of grass and sat down under the Bodhi tree and vowed not to rise from his meditation there until he had reached complete enlightenment. That's when Mara appeared."

"I remember!" shouted Briana. "He attacked the Buddha with

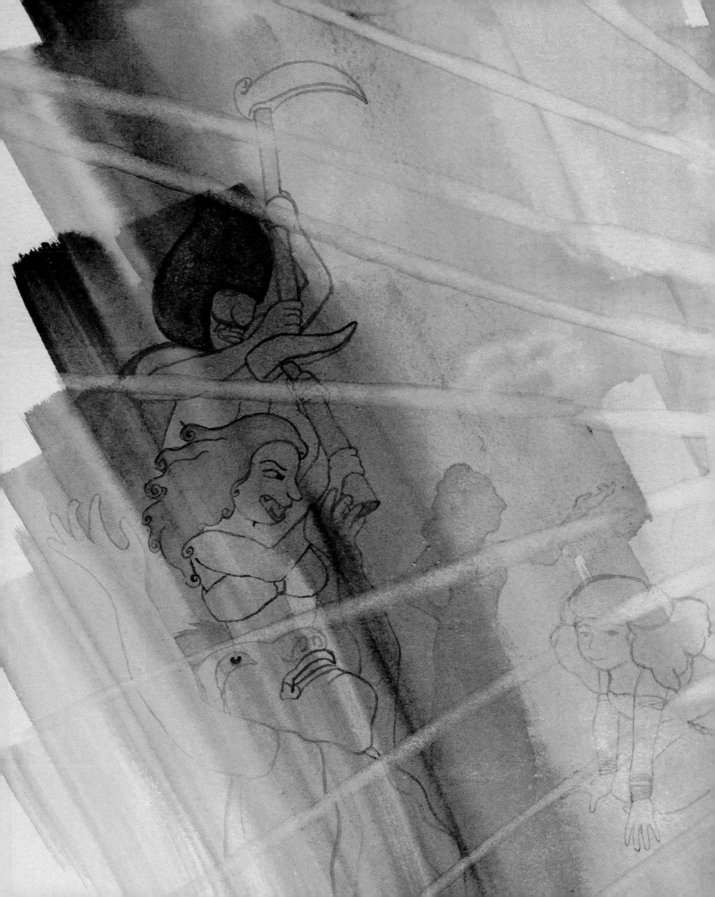

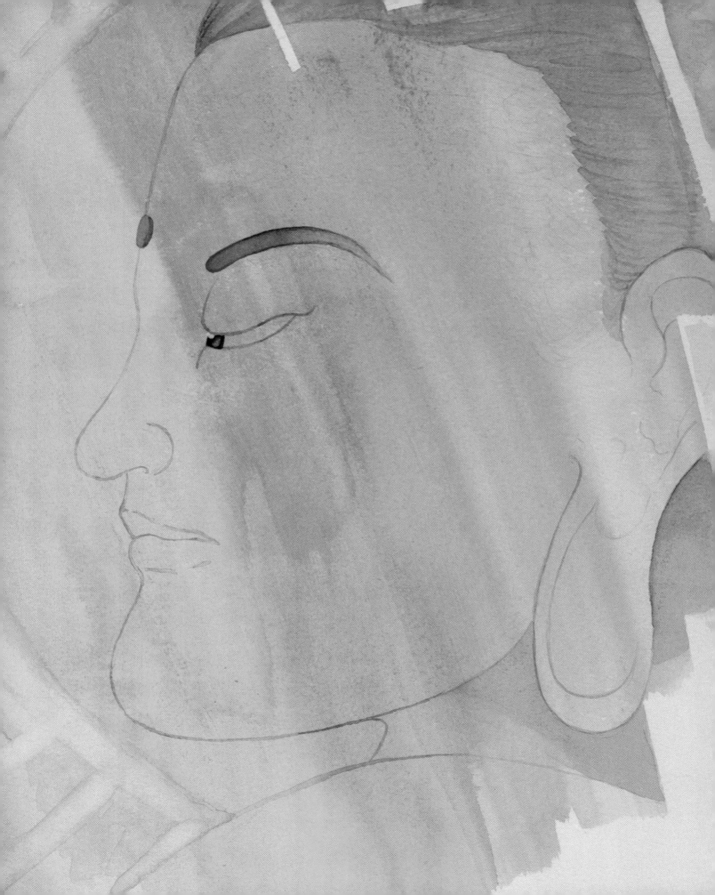

armies of demons and terrible monsters, all with horrible weapons and bloody fangs and wicked claws!" Briana hissed and growled and clawed at the air. One of the cats jumped up and ran for cover.

"That must have been pretty scary," said Papa.

"For most people it would have been," Mama agreed. "But was Siddhartha scared?"

"Nope," said Alex. "He just kept on sitting."

"Yep," said Briana. "And all the weapons and arrows turned into flowers."

"That's right," said Mama. "Siddhartha realized that Mara only had power over him if he gave Mara that power. When he didn't act on the fear and anger, the afflictive emotions just fell away."

"Then Mara sent his daughters," prompted Alex.

"Exactly. The daughters of Mara were very beautiful and represented all of the pleasures of life. They sang and danced and looked very lovely. But did Siddhartha join their dance?"

"No!" shouted Briana. "And then they turned into ugly old women and crumbled into dust!"

"Right," said Mama. "Siddhartha realized that change comes to all things. What seems beautiful and wonderful today will inevitably decay and fall apart over time. He had learned that lesson long ago back in the pleasure palaces. So when Siddhartha didn't desire or become attached to the daughters of Mara, they too simply fell away.

"But that wasn't the end. Mara still had one more attack to make and that was doubt. Mara himself appeared and demanded of

Siddhartha, 'What makes you so special? Why do you think you can attain enlightenment when so many others have failed?'

"And the Buddha said that he had accumulated merit over countless lifetimes by perfecting generosity, virtue, patience, diligence, concentration, and wisdom.

"'Who has seen you do these things?' shouted Mara. 'Who is your witness?'"

"'The Earth is my witness!'" shouted both children together.

"That's right!" said Mama. "Siddhartha touched the Earth as he said those words and Mara was finally defeated, falling away entirely. With no more obstacles to cloud his mind, Siddhartha attained full enlightenment, becoming Gautama Buddha, the Buddha of our age."

"Wow," said Alex.

"Cool," said Briana. "Come on, let's go play!"

The children ran off, Capewoman brandishing a sword from under her flowered cape; the Black Ranger flourishing a lightsaber from beneath a hooded robe.

"I am the great demon Mara!" yelled the Black Ranger.

"You cannot defeat me!" screamed Capewoman. "The Earth is my witness!"

Mama and Papa smiled at each other and went back to reading their books.

The Value of Persistence:
the story of Mahaprajapati

When Briana came home from school, her face looked like a rumpled blanket. "What's wrong, sweetheart?" Mama asked and the little girl couldn't stop the tears from spilling down.

"You look like someone who had a bad day," said Mama, gathering Briana up in a hug. "Let's go sit inside and you can tell me all about it."

As they entered the house, Alex came running up. "Hi Mom! Hi Brianna! I just heard what happened. I'm sorry they wouldn't let you play soccer."

His sister gave him an angry look through her tears. "It's none of your business!" she yelled. "Leave me alone!"

Mama gestured to Alex to follow them in. "Let's let Briana tell me what happened, okay?" She sat down and Briana climbed into her lap.

"Well, I wanted to play but Joey said I couldn't and I said why not and then Eric said it was because I'm in second grade, and no one wants to pick a little kid, especially if they're a girl."

"This was at recess?"

"Yes! Lots of kids want to play soccer at recess. Only there aren't enough spots so not everyone gets picked and I never get picked and it's not fair just because I'm little and I'm a girl!"

"You are kind of small," said Alex, who was getting his homework out of his backpack. "Maybe in a couple years when you're in fourth grade like me you can play soccer too."

"I am not small!" yelled Briana. "And I'm a really good player too, only nobody ever gives me a chance to show it!"

"You know," said Mama, "women through the years have faced all sorts of difficulties because people thought they couldn't do things as well as men could. Back in the time of Gautama Buddha, there was a woman named Mahaprajapati who faced just that problem, but she wouldn't take no for an answer."

"Did she want to play soccer too?" asked Briana.

"No, she wanted to become a nun. But when she asked the Buddha to ordain her, he refused."

"Just because she was a woman?" Alex exclaimed. "That's not fair - the Buddha should have known better!"

Mama smiled. "The Buddha was an enlightened being, but he was also trying to help people long ago in a very different historical time from ours. In that time, and in that part of the world, people didn't think it was such a great idea for women to shave their heads, put on simple robes, and leave the protection of their families to live outdoors and survive by begging."

"Begging?" repeated Briana, sitting up and staring at her mother. "Why would they have to beg?"

"Buddhist monks and nuns take many vows to help them renounce attachment to worldly things and develop spiritually. They don't have money or possessions like lay people do; they survive on the generosity of others. In the time of Gautama Buddha, that meant that they wandered from village to village, begging for food in order to survive."

"That sounds like a hard life," said Alex. "Why would anyone want to do that?"

"Because they want to follow the Noble Eightfold Path that the Buddha taught without the distractions of regular life. They want to attain enlightenment, find relief from the endless cycle of birth and death, and help all sentient beings be free from suffering."

"Oh, right," said Alex. "I forgot all that stuff."

Briana frowned. "Just because it's hard doesn't mean that women shouldn't be allowed to do it! If men can be monks, women should be allowed to be nuns!"

"That's what Mahaprajapati thought," said Mama. "She was actually both the aunt of Gautama Buddha and his stepmother; she had raised Prince Siddhartha from the time that he was just a tiny baby, when his mother died. So she knew all about why he had left the palace and that he had attained enlightenment and was teaching the Dharma to others."

"What's the Dharma?" asked Briana.

"The teachings of the Buddha," Alex told her. "So when did she ask the Buddha to become a nun?"

"Well, the Buddha had been accepting monks into the Sangha, or Buddhist holy order, for several years when he returned to his homeland to settle a water dispute between two neighboring kingdoms. The king, Siddhartha's father, was dead by this time. After the water dispute was settled, the Buddha stayed in the area to teach and he accepted many hundreds of men into the Sangha. Then Mahaprajapati and hundreds of women, many of them the wives or relatives of men who had just became monks, stepped up and asked the Buddha to ordain them also. However, the Buddha refused and left with the monks for the town of Vesali."

"That's just not fair!" yelled Briana. "Why wouldn't he let the women join?"

"Probably because of the reasons we talked about earlier. Women at that time were expected to stay at home and take care of their families. Other religions didn't allow women to become full monastics. Maybe the Buddha was worried about what other people would think about the new religion if he started encouraging women to leave the safety of their homes and embrace the religious life. Since monks and nuns cannot marry, maybe he was worried that it would cause problems to have both monks and nuns in the Sangha."

"That's still not fair," said Briana.

"Mahaprajapati agreed with you," said Mama. "So she told the women with her not to give up hope. They shaved their heads, put on yellow robes just like the monks wore, and walked all the way to Vesali, which was hundreds of miles away. When they arrived, their feet were all bloody and sore from walking so far and they were very tired. But Mahaprajapati was still determined. So she went to the Buddha again and asked to be ordained."

"And did he do it?"

"No, he refused again."

"Again?" yelled Briana. "She must have been angry!"

"She probably was very disappointed," Mama agreed. "But did she give up?"

"No!" cried Briana.

"You're right," said Mama with a smile. "What do you think she did instead?"

"Kept on asking?" suggested Alex.

"Well, sometimes when you ask one person for permission to do something and they say no, what might be a good strategy?"

"Ask someone else?"

"Exactly! Sometimes you need an ally. So Mahaprajapati went to Ananda, the Buddha's chief disciple and personal attendant, and she asked him to talk to the Buddha about allowing women to be ordained. Ananda agreed and went to see the Buddha, who refused to reconsider. But Ananda was just as persistent as Mahaprajapati! Finally, Ananda thought of a new way to ask the same question. He asked Gautama Buddha if women could attain enlightenment the same as men could, and the Buddha agreed that they could. 'Since women can attain enlightenment like men,' Ananda argued, 'then shouldn't they be allowed to be ordained like men?' And at that the Buddha finally agreed to ordain women, but only if they would agree to take eight more vows than monks take."

"That's still not fair," said Alex.

"It's certainly not equal," said Mama. "But it did allow the people at the time to accept the ordination of women. Mahaprajapati and the hundreds of women with her all became Buddhist nuns as a result. Later, Mahaprajapati attained enlightenment and did many wondrous things. And she was just the first; there are still Buddhist nuns and female teachers to this day. And many Buddhists, both female and male, are now trying to make sure that women have an equal place in Buddhist life."

"That's good," said Briana, laying her head on her mama's shoulder. "But I don't want to be a nun. I just want to play soccer!"

"A worthy goal," smiled Mama. "What do you think you can learn from Mahaprajapati's story to help you with your soccer problem?"

"Keep asking?" suggested Briana.

"Persistence and determination are definitely good lessons. But what else?"

"I could ask someone else to help me! Like maybe Mr. Whittaker, the recess monitor!"

"Now you're thinking," said Mama, giving Briana another hug. "Persistence, determination, and allies can help you succeed in almost any situation if you have a worthy goal."

In the Garden of Our Minds

When Alex came home from school, his face was as troubled as a stormy sky.

"What's wrong?" asked Mama. "Did you have a bad day?"

"I hate school! The teachers aren't fair and nothing fun ever happens!"

Briana said, "We can do something fun now. I'll play with you."

Alex flung his backpack on the ground and yelled at Briana, "Leave me alone!"

Briana began to cry. "That's mean!"

Mama looked around and saw cold dark shadows creeping into the house. *Where did all the sunshine go*, she wondered. "Everyone needs to calm down."

"I want to go outside and play," said Briana through her sniffles.

"Well you can't," said Alex. "It's windy and cold and starting to rain. I hate winter!"

"We could go to the garden of our mind," suggested Mama.

Briana stopped crying and Alex looked up.

"Follow me," said Mama and they did. Down the hallway, into the Buddha room.

When they reached the room, Briana yelled, "I want to ring the bell!"

"No - it's my turn!" shouted Alex.

"Calmly, quietly," said Mama. "What do we do before the bell?"

The children copied Mama's folded hands and three times recited with her the refuge prayer as they bowed to the shrine: *I take refuge in the Buddha. I take refuge in the Dharma. I take refuge in the Sangha.*

"Briana, you can invite the bell. Alex, you can say the breathing prayer."

The children sat like Buddhas on the floor as Mama brought out the bell that looked like a bowl.

"Dring..." sang the bell as Briana invited it. "Dring... Dring...."

Each time she let the previous sound fade away before inviting the bell again.

"Very good," said Mama, smiling at Briana, then Alex.

"I breathe in, I breathe out," Alex began, then hesitated.

"I breathe deep," helped Mama.

"I breathe slow," continued Alex.

"I am calm, I am at ease.

"I smile, I release.

"This present moment is a wonderful moment."

They all breathed quietly for a moment.

"Where's the garden?" asked Briana.

"I bet it's about the seeds," said Alex.

Mama smiled. "What do we say about the seeds?"

Alex's forehead wrinkled with concentration as he recited:

"I know that there are in me seeds of Buddha and seeds of Mara.

"I will help the seeds of Buddha in me to grow.

"I know that there are in my family seeds of Buddha and seeds of Mara.

"I will help the seeds of Buddha in my family to grow.

"I know that there are in all sentient beings seeds of Buddha and seeds of Mara.

"I will help the seeds of Buddha in all sentient beings to grow.

"But what does it mean?" asked Alex.

"Each of us," said Mama, "is a garden."

"Does that mean that flowers will grow out of my head?" giggled Briana.

"Or apples out of my ears?" laughed Alex.

"No," said Mama. "It has to do with being virtuous. Do you remember what virtuous means?"

"Virtuous means making good choices," said Alex.

"That's right," said Mama. "So each of us is like a garden, because if you plant virtuous thoughts in your mind, you will do virtuous actions and have virtuous results. If you plant non-virtuous thoughts in your mind, you will do non-virtuous actions and have non-virtuous results."

The children still looked confused, so Mama continued.

"If I plant watermelon seeds in the garden outside, what will grow?"

"Watermelon!" both children cried out.

"If I plant pumpkin seeds, what will grow?"

"Pumpkins!"

"How about flower seeds?"

"Flowers!"

"Exactly. It is the same with the gardens of our minds."

"So if we plant Buddha seeds in our minds, then Buddhas will grow?"

Mama smiled. "A Buddha is someone who is enlightened, who sees things as they truly are. A Buddha is calm, wise, compassionate, patient, and peaceful. A Buddha feels loving-kindness for all sentient beings. We all have the capacity to become Buddhas.

"If we tend the Buddha seeds in the gardens of our minds, then we will grow more calm, wise, compassionate, patient, peaceful, and full of loving-kindness."

"What about Mara seeds?" asked Alex.

"Mara represents the emotions that get in the way of us helping our Buddha seeds to grow. If you plant Mara seeds in the garden of your mind, you will grow hate, anger, ignorance, fear, and suffering."

The children were quiet.

"Let's take a look around the garden of our minds," said Mama. "Close your eyes and see the garden.

"It is wide and spacious, with rich, dark soil. Look at all the plants and flowers. Some are big and tall because you planted them a long time ago and have tended them well. Some are very new and small - just little green shoots peeking out of the ground."

"They're so cute," said Alex. "Like they're waking up!"

"We should water them," said Briana. "Plants need water to grow."

"You're right," said Mama. "There are three kinds of water in this special garden. The water of our actions, the water of our speech, and the water of our thoughts."

"I've never heard of water like that!" said Alex.

Mama smiled. "Look at the beautiful flowers growing in Briana's garden. They grew from seeds of generosity that Briana planted a long time ago. She has watered them well - with generous actions, like when she shared the candy she got for her birthday, and with generous speech..."

"Like when I told Papa he could go first in the game!"

"Right. And with generous thoughts..."

"Like when I thought that when I grow up I'm going to help make sure everyone has enough to eat so they aren't hungry!"

"Exactly. And each time you did, said, or thought those things, these flowers in your garden got bigger and taller and stronger and more beautiful!"

Briana smiled and her face reflected the radiant glow of the flow - ers within.

"What about me?" asked Alex.

"Do you see that stand of bamboo in your garden? There's a stalk there for each sentient being you've helped. Remember yesterday when you caught the moth in your room and let it go free outside? That's how that stalk over there grew. And the week before that, when you told the kid at school not to step on the spider? See that little stalk fluttering in the wind? That's because of the spider!"

"And when I thought about wanting grandma and grandpa to be healthy and live a long time - I bet that's the stalk over there!" And Alex sat a little straighter, his back strong like the bamboo in his garden within.

"How do we know if we're helping Mara seeds to grow instead of

Buddha seeds?" asked Briana.

"Well," said Mama, "one good way to tell is that if you are peaceful and calm you are growing Buddha seeds and if you are full of afflictive emotions like anger or jealousy you are growing Mara seeds. If I quiet my mind, I can tell how I am feeling. When I feel angry, I feel like there is a storm in my belly. What does being calm feel like?"

"Being calm feels like a nice warm day with a playground to play on," said Alex.

They sat quietly for a moment, holding the image inside their minds.

"Can I do the closing bell?" asked Alex.

"Yes," said Mama. "But first, let's dedicate merit."

The children repeated with Mama:

I dedicate all the merit I have accumulated from this and all other virtuous actions to benefit all sentient beings so that they may attain complete enlightenment.

May I be free from suffering.

May my family be free from suffering.

May all sentient beings be free from suffering.

Alex invited the bell three times. When the last sound had faded away, he sprang up from the floor. "Come on, let's go play!"

"I want to be the Warrior Gardener Queen!" shouted Briana, running after him.

Mama smiled as she put away the bell.

May I be free from suffering.
May my family be free from suffering.
May all sentient beings be free from suffering.

The Doorway of Death:
the story of Kisagotami

"Rise and shine, oh children of mine," sang Mama in the morning, flipping on lights and opening doors.

"That rhymes!" said Briana.

"Go away!" cried Alex. "I don't want to get up. I'm staying in bed." He covered his head with his blanket.

"You know what they say," responded Mama. "Every end is a new beginning."

"So the end of sleep is the beginning of the new day!" shouted Briana.

"Exactly," said Mama.

"What about death?" asked a muffled voice from under Alex's blanket.

"What?" asked Mama.

"Death," said the muffled voice. "What's death the beginning of?"

"Well," said Mama. "Death is the end of one life and the doorway to the next."

Briana sang out, "Next life I want to be a bird!"

The muffled voice under the blankets said, "I don't want to die."

"Most people don't," said Mama softly. "Most people are afraid of change and death is probably the scariest change of all."

She walked over to the bed. "Death can also be very sad, especially when someone we love dies. You know, there's a story about how Gautama Buddha helped a woman who was so sad about the death of someone she loved that she almost went mad with the pain."

"Ooh, a story!" said Briana. "I want to hear the story!"

"Well," said Mama, "there was a woman named Kisagotami, and her little boy, her only child, had died."

"That's so sad!" said Briana.

"It was very sad," Mama agreed. "Kisagotami was simply devas-tated by the death of her son. She couldn't sleep and she couldn't eat and she wouldn't let anyone take the body of her little boy away for a funeral. She just wandered around, her face swollen and stained with tears and dirt. And everywhere she went she would show people the dead body of her little boy and beg them to give her medicine to bring her son back to life."

Briana made a sour face. "She walked around carrying a dead body and not washing? That's disgusting!"

"Well, she was very sad," said Mama. "Think about how you would feel if someone you loved died."

"Someone like grandma or grandpa," said the voice from under the blankets.

"Or like one of the cats," said Briana. "I'd cry and cry and not wash and go around everywhere carrying..."

The voice from under the blankets interrupted. "I'd feel like there's a big empty space in my chest and I can hardly breathe. Like the sun is covered by clouds forever, and there's never going to be music anymore. Like I lost something really important and no mat-ter how hard I look I can never find it."

Mama stroked the head hidden under the blankets. "That's right, that's how Kisagotami felt."

"So what happened?" asked Briana.

"Well," Mama continued. "She wandered around for a long time until finally someone told her that she should seek out the Buddha because he was so wise that he understood all things and could surely help her."

"Because he was enlightened!" exclaimed Briana.

"Exactly. So Kisagotami went to the Buddha and collapsed in front of him, she was so exhausted. Her voice was almost gone because she had been crying so much, but she showed him the body of her son and begged him to help her."

The muffled voice asked, "What did the Buddha do?"

"He told her that he could help her, but she had to bring him a mustard seed from a house where no one had died."

"What's a mustard seed?" asked Briana.

"A seed from the mustard plant that is used as a spice or to make mustard. It was a very common type of seed at that time," said Mama. "Well, Kisagotami was overjoyed. Her new hope gave her strength. She thanked the Buddha and rushed off, stopping at the first house she came to.

"'Please help me!' she said to the pretty young woman who answered the door. 'I need a mustard seed from a house where no one has died so that the Buddha can bring my little boy back to this life!'

"The young woman shook her head sympathetically. 'You are welcome to have a mustard seed, but my father died here last year. I wish I could help you.'

"Kisagotami nodded in disappointment and rushed on to the

next house.

'Please help me!' she cried to the man who answered the door. 'I need a mustard seed from a house where no one has died so that the Buddha can bring my little boy back to this life!'

"The man looked very sad when he heard Kisagotami's words. 'I wish I could help you, but my wife died here recently.' Kisagotami saw a sad dark-eyed little girl peeking around her father's legs. 'I'm sorry for your loss, thank you,' Kisagotami said and she went on.

"This time she walked until she saw a large house that looked like it held a prosperous family. Here, she thought, I will get what I need.

"At the rich house, an old woman servant answered the door. 'Please help me!' Kisagotami said. 'I need a mustard seed from a house where no one has died so that the Buddha can bring my little boy back to this life!' The old woman shook her head. "I'm afraid we cannot help you. The son of this family died here many years ago. Everyone was heartbroken. I know how terrible you must feel. Good luck in your search."

"All day Kisagotami went from house to house and everywhere she went people shook their heads sadly and told their own stories of loss and grief. A daughter had lost her beloved mother to death, a mother had lost her beloved daughter. A little girl was mourning the death of her pet bird, a little boy was grieving for his dead grandfather. Everywhere, everyone knew death.

"Finally at the end of the day, as the sun was beginning to set, Kisagotami relinquished the body of her son. Then she returned to the Buddha, who was sitting in meditation with other monks, just as he had been in the morning.

"'Well, Kisagotami,' he said. "Have you brought a mustard seed from a house where no one has died?'

"'No, Blessed One,' she said, kneeling before him. 'There is no such house. Every house has been visited by death. Everyone knows death, whether they are young or old, rich or poor. Neither youth, health, beauty, or wealth can prevent death. I understand now.'"

There was silence in the room.

Finally Briana said, "But the Buddha didn't help her!"

"Yes he did," said Alex, sitting up and uncovering his head. "He made her feel better."

"That's right," said Mama. "Kisagotami realized that she was not the only one affected by death. All living things will die someday, no matter how much we love them. But if we know that, we can live better, like by appreciating the people we are with, when we are with them. And by treating all living beings compassionately."

"What happened to Kisagotami?" asked Briana.

"She became a nun," said Mama, "and dedicated the rest of her life to practicing the teachings of the Buddha so that she could attain enlightenment and be free from the endless cycle of births, lives, and deaths."

"Cool," said Briana.

"Yeah," said Alex. "But I think we'd better have breakfast soon or we're going to be late for school."

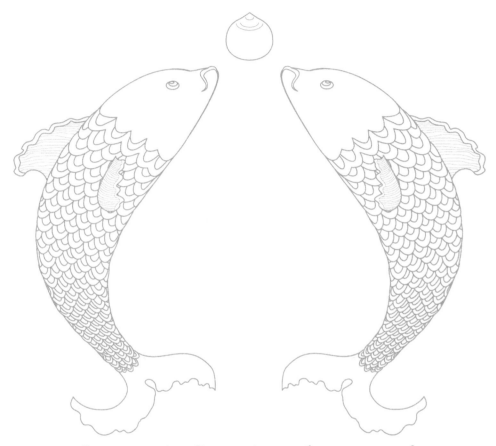

Lessons in Stopping: the story of Angulimala

When Mama came home from work, she was greeted by a chorus of voices.

"I got sent to the office!" yelled Briana.

"I forgot to bring my homework to school!" shouted Alex.

"I didn't finish my lunch!" cried Briana.

"Everyone quiet!" yelled Mama, who suddenly felt very overwhelmed. "I just came in the door and no one even said hello! I need to go change clothes. When I come out, I expect a proper greeting and I want each of you to tell me about three good choices you made today."

Mama went off to her bedroom, quietly repeating mantras. By the time she changed her outfit and washed her face, she was feeling much more peaceful and prepared to hear about the children's day at school. The children were feeling more peaceful and prepared as well.

"Good evening, Mama," said Alex very solemnly, when Mama entered the dining room.

Briana curtsied and bowed low. "Good evening, dearest mother. How are you doing this evening?"

"Quite well, thank you," said Mama, sitting down. "Good evening to you both. Look at this beautiful dinner! Thank you Papa for making dinner."

"Thank you Papa for making this beautiful meal," echoed Briana.

"Thank you magnificent Papa for using your precious time to cook this amazingly delicious dinner for us," said Alex.

"Right," said Papa. "You're all welcome. Dig in."

"So," said Mama. "Briana, tell me about three good choices you made today."

"Well," began Briana, "Today someone said something mean to me and I didn't say anything back, I just walked away. And then at recess I was playing soccer and a first grader wanted to play too and I shared the ball. And we had a movie in art because there was a substitute."

"How is that a good choice?"

"I paid attention and didn't talk too much."

"Very good," said Mama. "It sounds like you had some calm, generous, and focused moments today. Alex, how about you?"

"I finished all my math problems," said Alex. "And some kids were going to kill a cricket and I told them not to and I helped Mrs. Neil with moving the chairs for reading circle."

"Excellent," said Mama. "It sounds like you had some focused, compassionate, and helpful moments today. Now, what things do we need to work on?"

"Well," said Briana. "I got sent to the office."

"Why?"

"Well I was showing Jaena how my dress swirls when I spin and Mr. Tae told me to sit down at my desk and I didn't and then he told me to go to the quiet corner and I didn't and then he took me to the office."

Mama took a deep breath. "Okay, so what do you need to do so that doesn't happen again?"

"Stop talking, stay focused, don't talk when someone else is talking."

Briana rattled off a familiar list. "But it's too hard, Mama. I just can't stop myself from talking!"

"Sure you can," said Mama. "Remember what you said about art class - you watched the movie without talking."

"Yeah, but that was a movie. That was interesting. Spelling is boring. I can't not talk during spelling."

Mama closed her eyes for a moment. "You know, this reminds me of a story."

Alex groaned. "I bet it's another Buddha story."

"You're right," said Mama. "It's about the Buddha, but it's also about a terrible robber named Angulimala, who killed people and chopped off their fingers to hang on a gruesome necklace that he wore."

"Ooh," said the children.

"You're going to tell this at dinner?" asked Papa.

"Sorry," said Mama. "I'll wait until we're finished eating."

"Please?" begged the children. "Please tell the story now!"

Mama smiled apologetically at Papa.

"Okay," sighed Papa. "Go ahead."

Mama began. "Once in the kingdom of Kosala there was a terrible robber named Angulimala. His name had a special meaning. It's made of up two words - anguli and mala. Do either of you remember what a mala is?"

Briana raised her hand.

"Yes, Briana?"

"It's a prayer necklace."

Mama smiled. "Yes, we usually use the word mala to mean the string of 108 beads that Buddhists use to count mantras. The word mala means necklace and the word anguli means finger, and so Angulimala means 'finger necklace'. Angulimala had made a vow to kill 1,000 people. Every time he killed someone, he chopped off one of their fingers and hung it from his gruesome necklace."

"But why?" asked Briana. "Why was he so mean?"

"Well, some versions of the story say he had a bad teacher who secretly hated him and wanted to get him in trouble. The teacher said that in exchange for teaching him, Angulimala had to pay him 1,000 fingers, each from a different person. This is another good lesson. It doesn't matter who tells you to do something bad, you shouldn't do it because you are the one who will suffer the con-sequences. It's in your own interest to always do the right thing, because you're the one who will have to deal with the karma you create from your actions."

"But what happened to the finger robber guy?" asked Alex impa-tiently.

"Angulimala," Mama said. "Well, he had gotten all but one of the 1,000 promised fingers. Everyone in the kingdom was terrified of him and no one was able to stop him. Finally the king of Kosala decided to assemble a large army to hunt Angulimala down. When Angulimala's mother heard this, she decided to make one last attempt to find her son and convince him to stop his murderous ways. So she set out along a jungle road where Angulimala often attacked people.

"Now, the Buddha, as an enlightened being, was aware of things happening everywhere and he knew that Angulimala was so sick with anger and hatred that he would kill even his own mother in order to complete his gruesome necklace. He also knew that this was the perfect opportunity to show Angulimala the error of his ways. So the Buddha started out for the same jungle road. People saw him going that way and begged him to stop, because they didn't want him to be killed by Angulimala. But the Buddha just smiled and kept on walking.

"Eventually, Angulimala saw his mother coming down the road. For a moment he hesitated, but his mind was so clouded by anger and hate and his desire to be finished with the 1,000 fingers that he decided he would kill her. Then, just as he made his evil decision, he also saw the Buddha coming down the road. Angulimala felt relief that he wouldn't have to kill his mother because now he could kill this monk instead.

"So Angulimala rushed out of his jungle hiding place and began to chase the Buddha. But then a strange thing happened. No matter how fast Angulimala ran, the Buddha was always just ahead of him. And not only that, but the Buddha wasn't doing anything more than just mindfully walking, while Angulimala was running as hard as he could. And yet he still couldn't catch up. Angulimala got more and more frustrated and exhausted, until finally he yelled at the Buddha to stop and stand still.

"The Buddha continued his slow, calm walking and said, 'I have already stopped. It is you who must stop.'

"Now Angulimala didn't understand what this strange monk meant. After all, the Buddha was the one who was slowly walking and Angulimala was the one who couldn't catch up, no matter how hard he ran. 'What do you mean?' he shouted. 'I am standing still and you are still moving!'

"The Buddha smiled. 'My mind is calm and still. I have stopped doing any harm to sentient beings. Your mind is racing with anger and hate and your actions are full of harm. Be calm Angulimala and know peace and love for all sentient beings.'

"Those words and the Buddha's example were enough for Angulimala to suddenly realize the horrible things that he had done and the terrible karma he had accumulated. He fell before the Buddha and the Buddha blessed him as a monk."

Mama stopped and ate some of her dinner, which was growing cold.

"But what about the king and the army?" asked Alex.

"Well, the king met with the Buddha before he set out with his army to hunt down Angulimala. The Buddha asked the king what he would do if he learned that Angulimala had embraced the Dharma and become a monk. The king said that he would be very surprised, but that he would respect him as he would any other monk. Then the Buddha showed him Angulimala, with a shaven head and wearing monk's robes, and the king bowed to him in respect."

"What about the finger robber? What happened to him?" asked Briana.

"Angulimala lived by the vows of a monk and he meditated and tried to atone for all the horrible things he had done. But he still had to deal with his negative karma. One day when he went out to beg for food, an angry mob attacked and almost killed him. When he returned to the other monks, the Buddha told him that due to his good deeds of renunciation his bad karma was ripening now instead of in a future life."

"What does that mean?" asked Alex.

"It means that if he hadn't changed his evil ways, when he died he would have been reborn in a terrible hell for a very very long time. Because he stopped killing and became a monk, he was able to work off his bad karma in this life instead."

"So what does this have to do with school?" asked Papa.

"Oh, that's right," said Mama. "I was telling this story for a rea-son. We were talking about how difficult it is sometimes to stop doing things we shouldn't, like talking during class. The story of Angulimala teaches us that we can stop doing any bad action, even really really bad actions, once we make the decision to start acting correctly."

"So it's never too late to make a change for the better," said Papa.

"Exactly!" said Mama. "The important thing is to stop doing what you shouldn't."

"I've stopped!" said Briana.

They all looked at her and she grinned. "I've stopped eating my dinner - because I'm all finished! Can I have dessert now?"

"Certainly," said Mama, grinning back. "Good actions earn good consequences."

A Visit with Rinpoche

"Rinpoche is coming, Rinpoche is coming!" Briana exclaimed happily as she danced around the house.

"It's very exciting," agreed Mama.

"What does Rinpoche mean again?" Briana asked, coming to a sudden stop.

Mama smiled. "Rinpoche means 'precious teacher' in Tibetan. A Rinpoche is a Buddhist teacher in the Tibetan tradition."

"I'm nervous," said Alex with a frown. "I don't think I want to go."

"It's okay to be nervous," Mama said. "But we're all going to go. We don't have a chance very often to all hear a Rinpoche teach the Dharma."

"Why doesn't Rinpoche come more often?" asked Briana, twirling into her coat.

"Well, he doesn't live near here and he has many students in many places across the world that he visits. We're just lucky that he comes here even once a year and that he gives a special teaching for children."

Alex reluctantly started putting on his shoes. "Other kids in my class go to church every week. How come we only go once a year?"

"Why do you think that is?" asked Mama.

Alex shrugged. "I guess because we don't go to the same church that they do?"

"That's sort of right," said Mama. "What religions are the children in your class?"

"Mostly Christian, I guess," said Alex. "And Jacob celebrates

Hanukkah so that means he's Jewish, right?"

"Right," said Mama.

"Sayeeda is Muslim!" said Briana loudly. "What does that mean?"

"Well," said Mama, "all of those are different religions. Just in your classes, you know kids who are Christian, Jewish, and Muslim. And what are we?"

"Buddhist!" both Alex and Briana said at once.

"Right," said Mama. "We follow the teachings of the Buddha. And there are a lot less Buddhists where we live that there are Christians, Jews, and Muslims. So we don't have as frequent an opportunity to gather together and practice our religion."

Alex frowned. "What if we don't know anyone who's there? And what if we do something wrong and everyone looks at us?"

"It'll be fine," said Papa. "Just watch what Mama does and do the same thing. We'll all be together."

"We'd better get going," said Mama. "We don't want to be late."

Mama double checked that she had everything they needed and they all quickly got into the car. Once everyone was buckled up and Mama and Papa had consulted over the map, Alex asked another question.

"Sarah says that when they go to church, they study the Bible. What's the Bible?"

"The Bible is the Christian holy book, though different parts of the Bible are also revered by members of other religions. When Jews go to temple, they study the Torah and when Muslims go to a mosque they study the Koran. Those are all holy books."

"Do Buddhists have a holy book?" asked Briana.

"A lot of them!" said Mama. "Buddhists have the *sutras*, which are collections of the teachings of Gautama Buddha, the *vinaya*, which describe the rules that monks and nuns live by, and the *abhidharma*, which are complicated analytical writings."

"That's a lot of different stuff," said Alex.

Mama laughed. "There's actually a lot more than that! Different schools of Buddhism study different texts. As Buddhists in the Tibetan tradition we have the *tantra*, which are prayers and practices relating to the different bodhisattvas and Buddhas, like Tara and Chenrezig. There are also commentaries and teachings by later Buddhist teachers, even ones who are living today like His Holiness the Dalai Lama and His Holiness the Gyalwa Karmapa."

Alex shook his head. "That's too many! How do you know what to read?"

Mama smiled. "There are some texts that almost all of the different Buddhist schools think are important to study, like the Heart Sutra. But this is one reason that it's so important to listen to a Rinpoche teach the Dharma whenever we have the chance. Rinpoche will talk about a particular teaching and that will give us guidance about what to study."

"What is Rinpoche going to talk about?" asked Briana.

"We'll have to wait and see," said Mama.

Papa turned the car into the parking lot of the recreation hall.

"This doesn't look like a temple," said Alex skeptically as he got out of the car.

"It's not," said Mama. "When Rinpoche comes to town we have to find a place to host his teachings. Sometimes we all meet in someone's house, or, if a lot of people are expected to come, we try to get a bigger space, like a church or a community center like this."

"Don't Buddhists have temples of their own?" asked Briana.

"Definitely," said Mama. "But only in places where there is a larger Buddhist community. We don't have enough Buddhists in our area to support a temple of our own."

"I wish we did," said Alex. "I don't like being the only Buddhist in my class. Some kids say it's not even a real religion."

"Well, that just means that they don't know very much about Buddhism," said Mama.

"Why can't we be Christian or Jewish or something normal?" said Alex.

Papa laughed. "In some parts of the world, like Japan and Thailand, there are more Buddhists than members of either of those religions. We just happen to live in a place where that's not true."

Mama nodded. "And we're Buddhist because we believe in what the Buddha taught. That belief doesn't change just because not everyone around us believes the same thing."

Briana grabbed Mama's hand as they entered the recreation hall.

"We take off our shoes here," Mama said, pointing at an area filled with shoes. The kids looked around as they followed her example.

There was a big cushioned chair raised up at the front of the

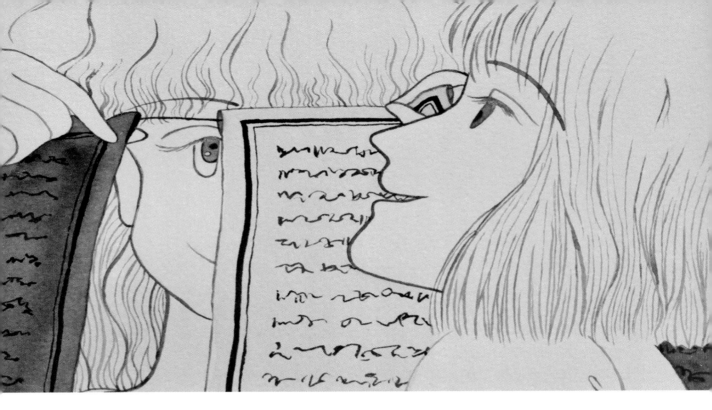

room with flowers all around it and a low table to one side. There were cushions and carpets laid out in rows before the chair; some people were already sitting down. Behind the big chair was a beautiful painting of a radiant white being with four arms. "Look!" said Briana, pointing at the painting. "We've got a picture like that in our house!"

"That's right," said Mama. "That's a thangka, a Tibetan Buddhist painting, of the bodhisattva Chenrezig. Isn't he beautiful?"

As they admired the painting, a woman came up to greet them.

"Hi!" she said with a warm smile at Alex and Briana. "Would you two like to help make a gift for Rinpoche?"

Alex hung back with Papa but Briana stepped forward. "Sure!" she said enthusiastically. "What do we do?"

"We're making a string of prayer flags for Rinpoche," the woman said, leading them all towards a craft area. "Do you know what prayer flags are?"

"Yep!" said Briana. "We have some on our porch. They're like colorful squares with prayers and pictures and stuff on them and when the wind blows, the prayers go out into the world!"

"Exactly!" said the woman with another smile. "So over here we have squares already cut out of yellow, red, green, blue, and white paper. Here are pictures of Buddhist symbols that you can cut out and paste on the prayer flags. Here are markers that you can use to write aspirations with. And then over here you can add your prayer flag onto the big string of flags that we're going to give to Rinpoche."

Briana followed along as the woman explained each of the areas. At the end she asked, "What's an aspiration?"

"It's a prayer or wish for other people," the woman said.

Mama stepped up. "Like if you say, *May all sentient beings be free from suffering*, that's an aspiration."

Briana nodded. "Let's get started!"

85

Alex and Briana worked hard to make their prayer flags beautiful. Alex picked out a piece of yellow paper and glued on pictures of the Buddha's eyes and the bodhisattva Tara. Briana chose pictures of a snow lion and a prayer wheel to glue on her piece of blue paper. Finally it was time to get Mama and Papa's help in writing aspirations.

"Okay," Papa said to Briana, "what do you want to say?"

"That all sentient beings should have long lives and not have suffering and everyone should have enough food and no one should die and..." Papa raised his hand to stop the torrent of Briana's words.

"How about you just choose one aspiration for each side," he suggested.

Briana considered this for a moment. "Okay, long lives and enough food," she said and Papa carefully wrote out *"May all sentient beings have long lives"* on one side and *"May all sentient beings have enough food to eat"* on the other.

Meanwhile, Mama was helping to spell words for Alex as he wrote down his aspirations: *"May all sentient beings know right from wrong"* on one side and *"May all sentient beings have a friend in their time of need"* on the other.

Once everyone was finished, Papa helped Alex and Briana tie their prayer flags to the long string that other children had helped to make.

"We should probably get a cushion," said Mama when they were done. "It's starting to fill up."

They found four cushions together and sat down carefully.

"Look at me!" cried Briana, pointing at her feet, which she had placed flat on the thighs of her opposite legs. "I can sit just like a Buddha!"

"That's called the lotus position," said Mama with a smile. "Very good. You're quite flexible."

"It hurts when I try to do that," complained Alex, who was struggling to lower his knees while his legs were crossed.

"Well, if you can get just one foot in position, that's called a half-lotus," said Mama. "But if you can't do that, then just sit in the chrysanthemum position."

"What's the chrysanthemum position?" asked Alex.

"The Buddhist master Thich Nhat Hahn uses that term to describe whatever position you feel comfortable meditating in," said Mama with a laugh. "I'm really good at the chrysanthemum position!"

"So am I!" laughed Alex.

"Quiet!" hissed Briana. "Here comes Rinpoche!"

Everyone quickly stood up and turned toward the door as an old monk in maroon robes entered, smiling at everyone and spinning a large prayer wheel. Alex and Briana copied Mama as she folded her hands and made a partial bow in the direction of Rinpoche, who moved slowly through the room and climbed up into the high cushioned chair. Once he was sitting, everyone did three prostrations in his direction: putting their folded hands at their forehead, throat, and heart and then kneeling down to touch their foreheads to the floor.

"That means we take refuge in the Buddha, Dharma, and Sangha," said Alex to Briana.

"I know that!" Briana said.

"Quiet you two," said Mama, as everyone sat back down on their cushions.

Rinpoche talked for a few moments to a young woman who sat down cross-legged behind the small table to his side.

"Who's that?" Briana asked.

"Next to Rinpoche's throne?" asked Mama. "That's the translator. Rinpoche will speak in Tibetan and she will translate what he says into English."

After everyone had gotten settled, Rinpoche began to speak in Tibetan, his deep voice rising and falling as he ceaselessly turned his large prayer wheel.

"What's he saying?" whispered Briana.

Mama shook her head. "Quiet and patience, Briana. We have to wait for the translator."

Finally, Rinpoche stopped talking and the translator began to speak in English. "Today Rinpoche is going to talk about what is a bodhisattva. A bodhisattva is a great hero who lives with a heart of love for all sentient beings. A bodhisattva is someone who has generated bodhicitta, or the mind of love for all sentient beings. A bodhisattva is someone who has made a vow not to pass into enlightenment until all sentient beings are enlightened first."

"Wow," said Briana. "That's hard."

"Each of us has the capacity to become a bodhisattva," continued

the translator after Rinpoche had spoken for a while again. "Every sentient being has a pure mind, a beautiful mind that is as clear as the cloudless sky. Our true nature is obscured, however, by the afflictive emotions of ignorance, attachment, and craving. These poisons are like clouds moving across the blue sky. The clouds do not change the pure nature of the sky, though they can hide it. Sometimes there are so many clouds coming and going in our minds that we lose sight of the clear sky underneath and forget that it is there. But just like a glass of river water that looks dirty when you stir it up and clean when you let it sit so that the silt can settle to the bottom, our pure mind, our enlightened nature, is always present."

The translator stopped and listened attentively as Rinpoche spoke again in Tibetan. When he had finished, she resumed her translation. "All sentient beings have this Buddha-nature, this potential to become fully enlightened and to benefit all sentient beings. When we keep our minds still and our hearts filled with love for all sentient beings, we can pacify the poisons of greed, hatred, ignorance, pride, jealousy, and doubt. These poisons are just like clouds passing across the sky. When you are mindful, you can see how they arise and cloud your pure mind, but they can never stain its fundamental nature. Cultivate the mind of love so that the obscurations settle like silt in the glass of river water, and your pure mind will be revealed, just like the great bodhisattva Chenrezig."

The translator paused again and now a younger monk, who had been sitting to one side, stood up and began handing out small yellow booklets to everyone present. The translator explained. "You are each getting a copy of The *Thirty-Seven Practices of Bodhisattvas*, which explains how a bodhisattva acts and lives. This is a very good text that you can read and study with your parents. You can also read the *Guide to the Bodhisattva's Way of Life* by Shantideva to learn more about the cultivation of bodhicitta and the perfections. Now we will learn the mantra of Chenrezig, which we can repeat as a practice to develop mindfulness and cultivate bodhicitta, the mind of love for all sentient beings. Let us all say with Rinpoche: *Om Mani Padme Hum*."

"I know this one!" exclaimed Briana. Everyone began to repeat the mantra, following the cadence set by Rinpoche. A feeling of love and peacefulness settled over everyone in the room.

When the mantra recitation was over, Mama stood up and gave Alex and Briana each a thin white scarf that she had in her bag. "This is a kata, an offering scarf," she explained. "We're going to get in line over here and when you come before Rinpoche, you put your hands in the prayer position, lay the kata across your wrists like this, and present the kata to Rinpoche with a bow. He will then move the kata around your neck and touch his forehead to yours. It's a sign of respect to Rinpoche and a blessing to you."

After the children had presented their katas and had their pictures taken with Rinpoche, Mama and Papa gathered up their things and everyone put their shoes back on at the door. There was a light rain falling outside and the world seemed hushed and peaceful.

"I'm glad we went," Alex said when they had gotten into the car and buckled up. "I was really nervous, but now I just feel happy."

"Me too!" said Briana. "Happy and excited because there's so much to do!"

"To do?" Papa repeated. "What else do we have to do today?"

"We have to go home and start cultivating the mind of love!" exclaimed Briana. "All sentient beings are depending on us!"

Glossary of terms

Afflictive emotions: negative emotions like anger, pride, selfishness, jealousy, greed, and doubt, which cloud our minds and make it difficult for us to see clearly and make good choices. The afflictive emotions are rooted in ignorance, attachment (desire), and aversion (hatred), which are often called the Three Poisons.

Bodhicitta: the mind of love for all sentient beings; the virtuous desire to bring happiness to all sentient beings and to help all sentient beings be free from suffering; the aspiration of bodhisattvas.

Bodhisattva: someone on the path to full enlightenment who promises to remain in the world until all sentient beings are enlightened first; someone who has perfected bodhicitta, the mind of love for all sentient beings. Two widely known bodhisattvas in the Tibetan tradition are Chenrezig and Tara.

Bodhi tree: the tree in Bodhgaya, India, under which Siddhartha meditated and attained enlightenment, becoming Gautama Buddha.

Buddha: one who is awakened or enlightened. The Buddha of our time is Gautama Buddha, who was born about 2,500 years ago in what is now Nepal and who attained enlightenment in Bodhgaya, India.

Buddha-nature: the potential of all sentient beings to become fully enlightened Buddhas.

Dharma: the teachings of the Buddha.

Enlightenment: realization of ultimate truth; the end of suffering.

Four Noble Truths: the fundamental teaching of the Buddha, which explains that:
(1) everything in life is constantly changing, which is why suffering is everywhere;
(2) the origins of suffering are the afflictive emotions;
(3) it is possible to end suffering by abandoning the afflictive emotions; and
(4) the way to abandon the afflictive emotions is to develop wisdom and virtue through the Noble Eightfold Path.

Gautama Buddha: the Buddha of our time.

Karma: the results of our thoughts, speech, and action. Positive karma, called merit, brings positive consequences (happiness) to our present and future lives. Negative karma, which comes from making bad choices based on the afflictive emotions, brings negative consequences (suffering) to our present and future lives.

Mala: a string of 108 beads used by Buddhists to count prayers and mantras.

Mantra: One or more sacred words usually associated with a particular bodhisattva; the mindful repetition of a mantra can help to make positive transformations in the mind. The mantra associated with the bodhisattva Chenrezig is Om Mani Padme Hum. The mantra associated with the bodhisattva Tara is Om Tare Tuttare Ture Soha.

Mara: a demon who personifies the afflictive emotions; Mara and his daughters are said to have attacked and tempted the Buddha when he was sitting under the Bodhi tree, trying unsuccessfully to prevent the Buddha from attaining enlightenment.

Merit: positive karma earned through good thoughts, speech, and action, like those based on the perfections of generosity, virtue, patience, diligence, concentration, and wisdom.

Mindfulness: being fully aware of the present moment, rather than distracted by the past, the future, or the afflictive emotions.

Noble Eightfold Path: the way to reach enlightenment through practicing right view, right aspiration, right speech, right action, right livelihood, right effort, right mindfulness, and right concentration.

Rinpoche: "precious teacher" in Tibetan; a title of respect for a Buddhist teacher in the Tibetan tradition.

Sangha: the Buddhist holy order (all of the Buddhist monks, nuns, and teachers) or, more broadly, all practicing Buddhists.

Siddhartha: the name of the Indian prince who would become Gautama Buddha.

Three Jewels: the Buddha, the Dharma, and the Sangha.

Conversations with Children

This section is intended to assist parents and discussion group leaders in facilitating conversations with children about the stories in this book. At the beginning of each story is an illustration of one of the Eight Auspicious Symbols, which are popular in the iconography of Mahayana and Vajrayana, or Tibetan, Buddhism. Each of the discussion segments that follows has a short explanation of the meaning of the related auspicious symbol and then suggests a few questions for discussion.

The short Dharma practice and guided meditation presented in the story *In the Garden of Our Minds* is intended for actual practice with children of almost any age. Everyone participating takes refuge, calmly breathes along with the "In, Out" poem inspired by Venerable Thich Nhat Hanh's mindfulness verse, and recites the lines about the seeds of Buddha and the seeds of Mara. The guiding adult can then invite each child in turn to "take a look around the garden of your mind". Encourage each child to state one recent action, speech, or thought that "watered" the child's Buddha seeds into flowers or plants in the child's mental garden. Keep the practice short so that everyone has a chance to participate and an atmosphere of calm reflection can be maintained. Once every child has shared, dedicate the merit of the practice to benefit all sentient beings. At that point, one of the other stories in the book can be read and a few of the suggested questions below used to spark discussion.

Table of contents
Auspicious symbol: Dharma wheel

The Dharma wheel symbolizes the Buddha's teachings. Modern Buddhism encompasses many different practices and beliefs, but certain teachings are common to all. These include respect for the Three Jewels of Buddha, Dharma, and Sangha, and study of the Four Noble Truths that explain the nature and origins of suffering, and how to end suffering through following the Noble Eightfold Path. Children are more likely to remember these concepts if they are presented multiple times in an interactive fashion, such as by discussing how the Four Noble Truths relate to each story in turn.

Prince Siddhartha Renounces the Throne
Auspicious symbol: precious umbrella

The precious umbrella symbolizes the activity of protecting beings from illnesses, obstacles, and harm. Just like an actual umbrella can protect someone from driving rain or the harsh rays of the sun, the umbrella of the Dharma can protect beings from suffering in this and future lives. Knowing that suffering has a cause and that there is a way to end suffering is very empowering.

Why didn't Siddhartha's father want him to become a great spiritual leader? Why do you think that Siddhartha was unhappy even though he had everything he could possibly desire? In what ways is modern life like life in Siddhartha's pleasure palace? What experiences have you had that have changed how you understand life?

Fighting the Demon Mara

Auspicious symbol: victory banner

The victory banner symbolizes the victory of the Buddha and his teachings, the Dharma, over the harmful forces and obstacles represented by Mara. Whenever you or someone else is inspired to act or speak in a way that is generous, virtuous, patient, diligent, focused, or wise, you can think that a banner is waving triumphantly to represent victory over the afflictive emotions, like selfishness, anger, laziness, or doubt.

When have you seen Mara lately? When have you seen the Buddha? Is it easier to avoid taking the afflictive emotions personally when you realize that change comes to all things? What are some ways that each of us can defeat Mara in our everyday life?

The Value of Persistence (the story of Mahaprajapati)

Auspicious symbol: treasure vase

The treasure vase symbolizes the limitless fundamental nature of our minds, filled with qualities like health, wealth, long life, prosperity, and wisdom. Even though we may face many obstacles in our lives, we all contain within ourselves the ultimate treasure vase: Buddha-nature. Enlightenment, the end of suffering, is a goal that can be pursued and attained in time by every sentient being.

Why do you think that people often focus on the differences between sentient beings (like gender, color, or religion) rather than the similarities? Why do you think that Mahaprajapati was so determined to achieve her goal of becoming a nun? Think about what happened to Briana in the story. What have you done when you've faced adversity in your life?

In the Garden of Our Minds
Auspicious symbol: eternal knot

The eternal knot symbolizes the interdependence of all things. Nothing stands alone and even things that at first look like opposites are interrelated. For instance, religious life and secular life might seem to be very different from each other, but they are fundamentally related, just like cause and effect, teachings and practice, wisdom and compassion. From the rain and the sun to the sentient beings living all over the world, everything is dependent on everything else.

Ask the children how they know when they are feeling calm. How is this calm feeling different from one of the negative feelings, like feeling angry, sad, or jealous? What are some ways that we can transform our "Mara feelings" into "Buddha feelings"? How can we help to grow the "Buddha seeds" in our friends and family? How does the calmness of our mind affect those around us?

The Doorway of Death (the story of Kisagotami)
Auspicious symbol: conch shell

The conch shell symbolizes how the Dharma sounds out deeply and powerfully to reach all beings and awaken them from ignorance. The Dharma is so pure and melodious that it can awaken even beings who are consumed by their suffering. While each of us may sometimes feel that we are all alone, in reality we are connected to everyone else. Realizing that everyone else experiences suffering too can help us develop compassion both for ourselves and for others.

Why did the Buddha tell Kisagotami to bring him a mustard seed from a house where no one had died, rather than just telling her that her little boy couldn't be brought back to this life? What can we do to help someone who has lost a loved one? Do you have any experiences with death that you would like to share?

Children's experiences with death may be vastly different. Some may have never personally known anyone who has died; others may have experienced the loss of a pet or close relative. Some children may be very comfortable in sharing their experiences, others may break down in tears, and some may express their discomfort through jokes or silliness. The breathing poem contained in the In the Garden of Our Minds story can be used to redirect and calm any agitation or inappropriate behavior. Most important is that anything shared or discussed in the group should be received compassionately.

Lessons in Stopping (the story of Angulimala)
Auspicious symbol: two golden fish

The two golden fish symbolize how practitioners of the Dharma are fearless even though they are surrounded by suffering, just like fish who swim through very deep water are not afraid of drowning. We may think that the fearlessness of the Buddha in this story is beyond anything we could ever do. However, fear and bravery are both just states of mind. Enlightened beings like the Buddha have complete control over, and awareness of, their minds. The Buddha taught that every sentient be-ing has Buddha-nature and can attain enlightenment through the Noble Eightfold Path, even people who have made a series of truly bad choices.

Why did Angulimala finally change his terrible behaviors? Think about a time when you tried to change one of your own behaviors. Were you successful in making a lasting change? How can we make changes in our behavior more likely to succeed? How might the lessons learned by Mahaprajapati help us? How can we oppose someone's bad behaviors but still have compassion for the person?

A Visit with Rinpoche
Auspicious symbol: lotus

The lotus symbolizes a completely pure body, speech, and mind. Even though a lotus' roots are sunk deep in mud, the beautiful flower rises unspoiled from the water. No matter where we start from or what has happened to us, we all have Buddha-nature and the capacity to purify our body, speech, and mind.

How would you explain Buddhism to someone who'd never heard of it? What does being a Buddhist mean to you? What does it mean to say that the afflictive emotions are like clouds passing across the clear blue sky? How can we keep developing compassion for others? What are some ways that we can help to develop love for all sentient beings?

About the Author and Illustrator

Michelle L. Johnson-Weider is a Buddhist in the Karma Kagyu Tibetan tradition who also practices with the Still Water Mindfulness Practice Center in the tradition of Thich Nhat Hanh. She is a lover of books, quilting, and Bollywood movies. Michelle lives in Maryland with her husband Kirk, their two children, and two cats. Kirk and Michelle also write fiction together as K.M. Johnson-Weider.

Brian Chen is also a Buddhist in the Karma Kagyu Tibetan tradition. He has studied and worked as an artist and graphic designer both in Taiwan and the United States. Brian can be reached at mindwaken@gmail.com

For more information about the book, including ordering information, visit 50percentdakini.com

ༀ་མ་ཎི་པ་དྨེ་ཧཱུྃ

Om Mani Padme Hum